v

Atlantic Ocean

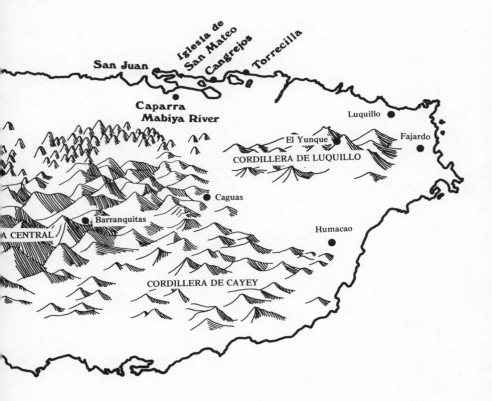

San Juan

Iglesia de San Mateo

Cangrejos

Torrecilla

Caparra
Mabiya River

Luquillo

El Yunque

Fajardo

CORDILLERA DE LUQUILLO

Caguas

Barranquitas

A CENTRAL

Humacao

CORDILLERA DE CAYEY

Sites mentioned in the legends in bold type.

Rico

Puerto Rican Tales

Legends of Spanish Colonial Times

By Cayetano Coll y Toste

Translated and Adapted by
JOSE RAMIREZ RIVERA

Ediciones Libero
Mayagüez, Puerto Rico

1st Edition—July 1977
2nd Edition—Dec. 1977

Second Printing, revised, January, 1979
Third Printing, November, 1980
Fourth Printing, October, 1988
Fifth Printing, revised, January, 1994

ISBN: 0-9601700-3-0
Library of Congress Catalog No. 78-108190

EDICIONES LIBERO
Betances Este 166
Mayagüez, Puerto Rico 00680

Illustrations: Janet Slemko, Brad Klein

Printed in the United States of America

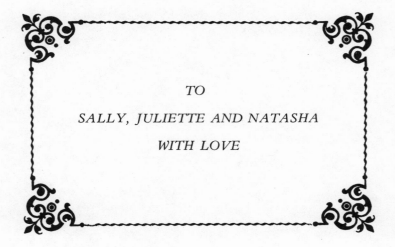

TO

SALLY, JULIETTE AND NATASHA

WITH LOVE

TABLE OF CONTENTS

Map of Puerto Rico   iv

FOREWORD – *in English and Spanish*   xiii

PREFACE   xvii

TALES OF ADVENTURE

The Gold Nugget   2
The Shark Killer   7
Roberto Cofresí: The Pirate   14
Carabalí: The Rebellious Slave   19

TALES OF ROMANCE

Guanina   30
The Diamond Ring   41
The Daughter of the Executioner   45

HISTORICAL TALES

A Good Toledan Sword   56
The Eleven Thousand Virgins   61

TALES OF RELIGION AND SUPERSTITION

The Miracle of Hormigueros   67
The Church of Christ the Healer   70
The Bell of the Sugar Mill   72

HISTORICAL NOTES   80

IMPORTANT HISTORICAL EVENTS   84

Map of Old San Juan   87

ABOUT THE AUTHOR   89

FOREWORD

Literary translation as an art form dates more than one hundred years in the history of Puerto Rican Literature. Those who have cultivated it compose a growing list of illustrious names: Betances, Baldorioty de Castro, Elzaburu, Amy — with them were initiated translations from English to Spanish and vice versa. Carmela Eulate Sanjurjo, Guerra Mondragón, José Antonio Dávila, Angel Flores, Gadea Picó, César Abdallah Portala, Arriví, Pedro Juan Soto, René Marqués, to mention only a few, stand out for the quantity and quality of their writings. The contributions of these authors greatly aid in presenting outstanding literary achievements in the French and English language to the Puerto Rican intellectual awareness. They also lend momentum, mainly through English translations, to the dissemination abroad of more than a few of our most noteworthy Puerto Rican literary creations, particularly those belonging to the last three generations of the current century — namely the generations of the thirties, the mid-forties and the sixties — not to exclude some choice selections from nineteenth century authors.

A recent demonstration of the translations taking place in this country is the English version of a selection of historical legends penned by Doctor Cayetano Coll y Toste appearing in this volume. This is realized by a contemporary physician, Doctor José Ramírez Rivera, who enthusiastic as the former was with literary endeavours, transcends the boundaries of his profession. Unquestionably, this translation is a very fitting and lovely tribute bestowing thanks and admiration from this young contemporary physician to the venerable and prestigious figure of his colleague of the past. Dr. Coll y Toste, besides exercising his noble profession, gave as his inheritance to Puerto Rico a voluminous and priceless literary and humanistic work involving various fields — historiography, narrative prose, poetry and others. And, incidentally, it also included, in some instances, translation: we owe to Coll y Toste a free verse translation of Edward Fitzgerald's fifth English version of the *Rubaiyat of Omar Khayyam*. This translation was published in the famous *Revista de las Antillas*, edited in San Juan in the years 1913-1914 by the illustrious poet Luis Lloréns Torres.

The *Puerto Rican Tales* (1924-1925) were the climax of Coll y Toste's work in the literary field. They transcend time by the endearing patriotic sense and sentiment they breathe. They make perfect continuity in spirit and form with the style of the historical legend which had its beginning and reached its highest realization in Hispanoamerican literature with the famous *Peruvian Traditions* of Ricardo Palma. The narrative in some of these stories is based on a series of precise historical events which Coll y Toste himself investigated and clarified successfully. The others are gathered from the medley of traditional legends framed within the long Spanish colonial period of four centuries, from the sixteenth through the nineteenth. There have been many generations of Puerto Rican students who have learned in their time, and, in large measure, to know and value the historical past of their native land by the indirect road of the events and unforgettable historical characters introduced by Coll y Toste in his stories. Today, many Puerto Ricans live away from the island, in self-imposed exile, in various cities in the United States—New York, Newark, Chicago and others— in search of rosier opportunities for life and work. Their children, often born in those regions, frequently grow in partial or absolute ignorance of Spanish, even though they show an active interest in reaching their Spanish and Antillian cultural roots. This collection of legends translated in English will doubtlessly serve our compatriots as an effective means to delve into the same historical source offered to those of us who were raised in Puerto Rican classrooms, reading the original Spanish version of the stories of Coll y Toste. The simple, but elegant and pleasant prose of the illustrious Puerto Rican writer and historian does not lose its essential qualities in the English version offered in these pages. The translator has successfully surmounted the multiple obstacles presented by linguistic expressions with the sharpest insular Puerto Rican flavor. He has tried to preserve unaltered in his English version (and does it most effectively) not only the genuine general expression of the author he translates, but also the characteristic, unfurbished prose in its original native form.

For what has been stated above we congratulate wholeheartedly the author of these translations. All Puerto Ricans conscious of our cultural heritage rejoice unabashedly in his achievement.

Manuel Alvarez Nazario
Professor of Hispanic Studies
University of Puerto Rico
Mayagüez Campus

PROLOGO

El ejercicio de la traducción como labor de arte literario presenta hoy día un cultivo ya centenario en la historia de las letras en Puerto Rico, y agrupa en el conjunto general de quienes lo han practicado a una creciente lista de nombres ilustres: Betances, Baldorioty de Castro, Elzaburu, Amy — con quien se inician en el país las traducciones del inglés al español y viceversa—, Carmela Eulate Sanjurjo, Guerra Mondragón, José Antonio Dávila, Angel Flores, Gadea Picó, César Abdallah Portala, Arriví, Pedro Juan Soto, René Marqués, etc., para sólo mencionar a los traductores más destacados por el volumen y calidad de sus trabajos. La obra de estos escritores por la vía indicada contribuye en importante medida a traer al conocimiento del ámbito intelectual de Puerto Rico determinadas realizaciones sobresalientes en las literaturas de lenguas francesa e inglesa, y asimismo presta notable impulso, en alas del traslado principalmente al inglés, a la difusión por el exterior de no pocos de nuestros textos literarios puertorriqueños de mayor relieve, pertenecientes sobre todo a escritores de las tres generaciones últimas del siglo en curso —la del treinta, la del cuarenta y cinco y la del sesenta—, pero sin excluir algunas selecciones de mayor valor y significación por autores del XIX.

Como una última manifestación hasta la fecha de la traducción literaria que se efectúa en el país, aparecen ahora en este volumen las versiones al inglés de un conjunto selecto de leyendas históricas que se deben a la pluma del doctor Cayetano Coll y Toste, las cuales realiza otro médico en el presente, el doctor José Ramírez Rivera, entusiasmado como aquél, al margen de su misma profesión, de las labores en el campo de las letras. Resulta sin duda un muy apropiado y hermoso tributo de agradecimiento y admiración éste que rinde con sus traducciones el joven médico de hoy a la venerable y prestigiosa figura de su colega de ayer, quien a la par del ejercicio de su noble quehacer profesional supo legarle a Puerto Rico una voluminosa cuanto valiosísima obra de literato y de humanista, la cual abarcó el cultivo de varios géneros —historiografía, prosa narrativa, poesía, etc.—, y dicho sea de paso, incluyó también en algún momento el trabajo de traducción: se debe a Coll y Toste un traslado en metro castellano libre del *Rubaiyat de Omar Khayyam,* partiendo de la quinta versión inglesa del mismo que realizara Edward Fitzgerald, obra de traducción que se publicó en su día en la famosa *Revista de las Antillas,* editada en San Juan por los años de 1913-1914 bajo la dirección del egregio poeta Luis Lloréns Torres.

Las *Leyendas puertorriqueñas* (1924-1925) de Coll y Toste, punto culminante de su trabajo más propiamente literario, se salvan en alas del tiempo por el entrañable sentido y sentimiento patrios que alientan en ellas. En perfecto enlace de continuidad, por su espíritu y forma, con el género de la leyenda histórica que tuviera comienzos y su más elevada cima, en las letras de Hispanoamérica, con las famosas *Tradiciones peruanas* de Ricardo Palma, el relato se sustancia en dichas narraciones sobre una serie de hechos menudos documentados en la historia escrita del país que el propio Coll y Toste contribuyó a investigar y esclarecer con resultados de tanta magnitud, o bien se recogen del acervo de leyendas tradicionales enmarcadas en el amplio periodo colonial español de cuatro siglos, desde el XVI al XIX. Han sido muchas las hornadas de escolares puertorriqueños que han aprendido en el tiempo, en no escasa medida, a conocer y estimar el pasado histórico de la tierra natal por el camino indirecto de los episodios y personajes inolvidables que nos presenta Coll y Toste en sus relatos. Hoy día, cuando tantísimos puertorriqueños viven fuera de la Isla, en autoimpuesto exilio, en diversas ciudades de los Estados Unidos —Nueva York, Newark, Chicago, etc.—, a la búsqueda de más rosadas oportunidades de vida y trabajo, pero donde sus hijos, muchas veces nacidos por aquellos horizontes, crecen frecuentemente en el desconocimiento parcial o total del español, si bien mostrando siempre vivo interés por llegar hasta sus raíces culturales hispánicas y antillanas, este manojo de leyendas traducidas al inglés habrá sin duda de servir a tales compatriotas como medio eficaz para ahondar en el mismo conocimiento de la historia insular que nos brindó a los escolares que nos formamos en las aulas del país la lectura directa en la versión española original de las narraciones de Coll y Toste. La prosa sencilla pero elegante y amena del ilustre historiador y literato de Puerto Rico no pierde sus valores esenciales en la versión inglesa que aquí se nos ofrece en estas páginas. El traductor se ha esforzado, venciendo los múltiples escollos que le presentan las expresiones léxicas de más profundo sabor insular de Puerto Rico, por conservar inalterado en su traslado al inglés— y así lo logra con mucho acierto— tanto la autenticidad expresiva general del autor traducido, como el particular curso llano de la exposición prosística en su forma vernácula primera.

Por todo lo antedicho felicitamos muy calurosamente al autor de estas traducciones, y por su feliz realización nos alegramos sin reservas todos los puertorriqueños conscientes de nuestros valores culturales.

Manuel Alvarez Nazario
Catedrático de Estudios Hispánicos
Universidad de Puerto Rico
Recinto de Mayagüez

PREFACE

The twelve legends translated here are historically fla-
vored Caribbean vignettes which provide a pleasurable
perception of the Puerto Rican way of life of previous
centuries. Synoptic and humanly oriented, they give life
and substance to cut and dried events called by the
learned "history."

The translator undertook his task while an intellectual
expatriate in the city of Baltimore. He saw in his own
children the rising dilemma of those who may feel Puerto
Rican, but falter in Spanish. He felt that an early reading
of historical accounts such as these might help to re-
store a sense of identity and provide a stimulus to sample
more broadly their ancient heritage.

At the outset, it became clearly evident that a literal
translation would defeat this purpose. The lengthy sentences and complex syntax of nineteenth-century Spanish prose seemed unpalatable for a young reader. Although attempting to maintain the stylistic flavor of a
Spanish story, the translator took broad liberties in pouring the content into a more readable and relatively mod-
ern mold. Repetitious phrases have been deleted,
sentences shortened; whole paragraphs have been recast
to ensure coherence and reasonable continuity of
thought. Such broad literary license may seem unwar-
ranted to the scholar. The translator will be content if it
provides a readable story for English-reading youths who
want to sample our folklore.

The translator thanks Professor Samuel F. Febres and
Mr. Jim Billys Latoni for proofreading the manuscript.
Unlimited thanks are due to Dr. José Abreu Elias who
by his appreciation and example encouraged the publication of this work and who, in effect, engineered its
publication.

José Ramírez Rivera

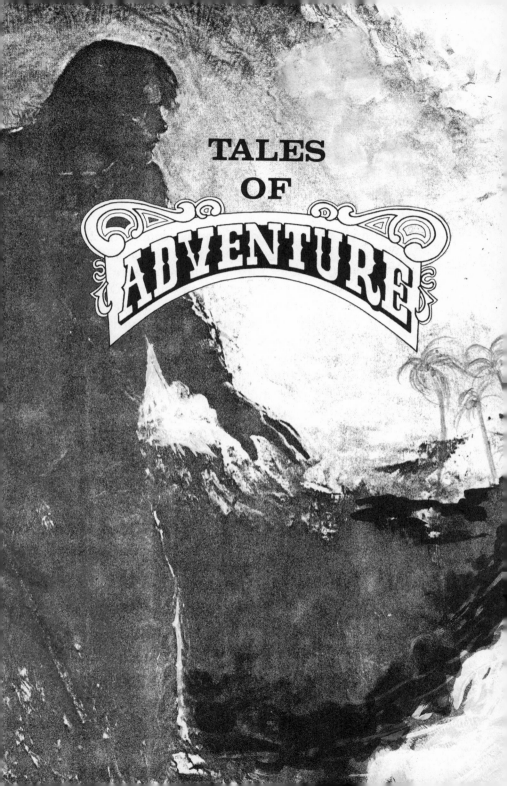

TALES
OF
ADVENTURE

The Gold Nugget
(1530)

Among the settlers of Boriquén[1] coming to the New World in search of gold, there were two ambitious and handsome young men from Seville who were very close friends, Antonio Orozco and Juan Guilarte. Orozco was about thirty, lanky, white-skinned and freckled, with small gray eyes. The aquiline nose betrayed his racial mixture of Vandal and Jew. He was impatient and daring; a cunning expression lurked in his face. Antonio Guilarte was a full-blooded Berber,[2] with dark skin, slanting eyes, and a fine straight nose. His smiling oval face ended in a curly black beard. He liked to make love to the Indian girls, who were amused by his bewitching guitar. They taught him to dance and sing Indian tunes.

The two men came to the island by royal charter, and settled in the capital city of Caparra. Each had a plot of land, a stable, and forty Indians who worked their gold claims at the Mabiya River, panning the sands in search of the shiny fragments.

One day, Orozco said to Guilarte, "Let's go inland and see if we can find a new source of gold. Let's go alone, with no guide except our compass. We can take a

1. Indian name for the Island of Puerto Rico
2. A member of a group of North African tribes from Barbary and the Sahara

few days' provisions and go south. The foremen can manage the gangs here on the Mabiya."

"A fine idea," agreed Guilarte. "Since we are to sleep in the woods, let's not forget our blankets to protect us from the morning coolness."

Orozco and Guilarte explored the virgin semi-tropical jungle for eight days until they arrived at a summit. From there they could see the Caribbean Sea on one side and the Atlantic Ocean on the other. It was a splendid panorama of turquoise stripes of sea on either side and hills and valleys in varying shades of green, from light emerald to agate.

"Beautiful," said Guilarte. "I wish we could build a summer cottage here."

"Don't be a fool," replied Orozco. "This view is good to be admired, but after a while it would grow tiresome."

"It would never tire me," muttered Guilarte as he gazed intensely down the green hills festooned by blue waters.

"Bah! This is the end of the world," continued Orozco. "The best thing we can do is to gather enough gold to return to Triana. From Seville to heaven, I say."

"For that, we must wash a lot of sand, my friend," said Guilarte, "especially when we have to give one-fifth of the gold to the King, just because he is King. God! It's going to take years to make a fortune."

The friends lingered on the hilltop. After a while they opened their knapsacks and began to devour tortillas made from cassava[3] and chunks of cottage cheese.

3. Manioc, a tuberous root

Suddenly, Guilarte pointed: "Look, look into that hollow, down to the left! Do you see anything?"

"Ah," breathed Orozco, "a stone shining like topaz in the rays of the sun."

"Look closer! It is a piece of gold fused to a chunk of quartz."

"I see it!" shouted Orozco, "It's really enormous."

"But who in the devil is going to go down there and pick it up?"

"Why, you and me, of course," said Orozco.

"That's fine to say, but how do we do that?"

"Well, we will camp here in your favorite spot and make ropes out of majagua.[4] If we reinforce the stems with vines, the ropes will make a good ladder. The palms are here and over there I can see a thick head of majaguas. There are vines everywhere."

"On with it then," urged Guilarte, moving eagerly. The golden rays of sunlight penetrating the unspoiled jungle had lost their glimmer to the shining gold.

The foliage near the abyss was sparse. From a bare rock a thin stream of cold water emerged; diving from rock to rock, it disappeared into the depths of the immense hollow. The two men weaved their ladder quickly and expertly. After securing it to a giant cedar tree, they descended down the steep and rocky slope into the valley. There the stone lay. It was even larger than they had imagined.

"Once separated from the quartz," said Guilarte, this nugget will be worth four or five thousand Castilians."[5]

---

4. A tropical tree
5. A small gold coin worth around seventy-five cents

"This is enough to make one of us rich, but not both of us," noted Orozco. "Let's look further for another." But they found no more gold.

"I have a deal for you," Orozco said. "Let's roll some dice. Whoever wins will have the gold and can retire at once to Spain. He who loses will stay at Caparra and exploit both claims for our common benefit."

"Good, throw the dice."

Chance favored Orozco, and Guilarte cheerfully congratulated him.

"Your wish is fulfilled. Now let's get back to the summit."

"Right," said Orozco, "you go first and I will follow you with the stone."

Guilarte climbed quickly up the ladder and sat at the edge of the cliff to wait for his friend. Orozco followed, getting about halfway easily. At that point, one of the rungs of the ladder broke, and Orozco nearly fell; his left hand was burdened with the gold-filled stone. "Pull the ladder up!" he shouted. "Hurry, or I will have to let the stone go!"

Guilarte, a robust man, pulled strongly and eagerly. But abruptly he fell backwards. The fiber ladder could not take the rough abrasion of the rock and broke. The unfortunate Orozco fell far into the hollow. He seemed to be hurt and unconscious.

Unable to help him, Guilarte walked day and night to the camp on the Mabiya River for assistance. Then with skilled Indians and a good ladder, he returned to aid his friend.

Orozco, barely alive, still clasped the stone. He first asked for water and then, before dying, whispered, "Guilarte, listen to me. I'm sorry. You found the gold nugget, and I took it from you with loaded dice. God has punished me. Forgive me."

Although Orozco fell victim to the master passion of greed, his body was brought for a Christian burial near the Mabiya River. Guilarte gave the enormous gold nugget to the Cathedral at Seville as a symbol of friendship broken and redeemed.

The King was notified, and he granted Guilarte all the land explored by him and his friend. Even today, in the central chain of mountains which divides the island, a summit called "La Sierra de Guilarte" reminds us of this tragic tale.

The Shark Killer

(1640)

The town of Aguada was bristling with holiday spirit. Spanish galleons carrying the Viceroy of New Spain and the Bishop of Tlasteca on their way to Veracruz had dropped anchor in the bay. While the fleet took aboard water and provisions, the noblemen went ashore.

The new Viceroy, Marquis of Villena and Duke of Escalona, wanted his visit to be remembered so he asked the local magistrate for a child to christen and protect. The child was christened Diego de Pacheco (the name of his illustrious godfather) by Don Juan Palafox y Mendoza, one of the Bishops of the retinue.

The governor of the island, Don Agustin de Silva, and the residing prelate, Alonso de Solis, came from the Capital to Aguada to welcome these important dignitaries at gay and magnificent celebrations which remain recorded in the chronicles of the island.

II

At the banquet honoring the representatives of His Majesty, Don Diego de Pacheco said, "Gentlemen, nothing has amazed me more on this long voyage than a frightening fish called a shark which I saw taken out of the sea two days before arriving at your shores. This fish was eleven feet long. It had a mouth lined with rows of moveable teeth. Even while lying dead on the deck of our ship, the wild beast was terrifying."

"Sir," boasted the local magistrate, "here in Aguada we have a man who fights sharks."

"My friend," exclaimed the amazed viceroy, "how can this be true? If this is so, I would be most pleased to witness such an encounter. Call this man, I would like to meet him."

III

Rufino was the shark killer. He lived across from the docks in the village of Aguadilla, and made his living as a fisherman. He was scarcely 20 years old, heavily tanned, short, compact, with broad shoulders and muscular arms. At a glance one could see in him the mixture of European and Indian races which populated the island. He had large black eyes, a hook nose, thick lips and bushy black hair. Rufino was not only friendly, but also humble and accomodating. At the town hall the following conversation took place:

"Young man, our noble guests wish to see you fight a shark. Are you willing?"

"No, sir."

"Why not?" asked the amazed magistrate.

"Because I don't have the scapulars[1] of the Virgin."

"And where are they?"

"They were worn out so I sent them to the Carmelite Convent in the capital to be repaired."

"I will give you four silver pesos if you will fight a shark tomorrow before the Viceroy and the Bishop who are on their way to Mexico."

"I cannot do it. I can't fight without the scapulars of the Virgin."

"I will give you eight pesos."

"It's impossible, sir!"

Rufino was presented to the Viceroy, who, having heard about the fisherman's decisive refusal, treated him cordially and spoke to him in his most persuasive manner.

"Tomorrow you will fight the shark, and I will add an ounce of Spanish gold to the eight silver pesos that the magistrate will give you."

IV

The shark killer was awake all night. It was his damnable luck, he thought. Now that he had the opportunity to earn a handful of badly needed money, he was without the scapulars of the Virgin. Without these, he had never gone to sea — not even to fish.

He arose early, looking for his knife, which he called "my pin." It was a large dagger, thirteen inches long, with a serrated blade one inch wide and a strong bone

---

1. A badge with a religious symbol consisting of two pieces of cloth joined by strings and worn under the clothing around the neck.

handle. After inspecting the strap used to secure the knife to his wrist before underwater combat, Rufino oiled the blade and returned it to its sheath. Then, impatiently, he left the house and walked towards the small town square.

The sea looked like a sheet of steel. It was dotted by Spanish galleons flying their colorful flags and fishing boats returning to port with their catch. After looking at the scene, Rufino turned abruptly and went into one of the neighboring cafés for breakfast.

V

By 10:00 a.m., a crowd had gathered at the beach. Soon thereafter the watchtowers announced that a shark had entered the bay. The local magistrate hastened to advise his noble guests, and the whole retinue headed towards the shore.

Rufino remained at the café. He sat at a table holding his head with both hands. The noise from the beach struck his ears like an insult. The shouting grew louder and louder: "Rufino! Rufino!"

When the café owner touched his shoulder, Rufino jerked his head up and asked angrily, "What is it?"

"Nothing, just that today you are going to earn a lot of money."

"I don't know . . . "

Then he anxiously rose from the chair and walked in the direction of the beach, where groups of people were gathering everywhere.

From the boat moorings, Rufino nervously scanned

the horizon. He clenched his fists in anger when he saw a black fin rising from the waves. On command of the magistrate, a dog was thrown into the waters to lure the hungry shark towards the shore. Suddenly the fin disappeared as the fish turned belly up to devour the luckless dog and a widening patch of red froth stained the blue waters.

Rufino had seen everything. His eyes flashed with rage and eagerness to fight the beast. He ran to the end of the dock, undressed rapidly and dove into the sea with the dagger strapped to his wrist. The crowd cheered.

When the sinister fin emerged, Rufino swam bravely in its direction. Suddenly both the fin and Rufino went under the reddening waters. Minutes passed before the young man reappeared swimming frantically towards the shore.

"My scapulars! My scapulars!" he muttered, before fainting.

The clamor was deafening. On the surface of the water, the outline of the lifeless beast was becoming visible. Fishermen in their little boats began to drag it towards shore.

Rufino, while stabbing the dying monster for the second time, was struck on the chest with such force that he almost lost consciousness. Had he fainted he surely would have drowned.

The Viceroy approached, placed his right hand on the head of the triumphant killer, and handed him two ounces of gold.

Suddenly both the fin and Rufino went under the reddening
waters.

"You are a man of courage," he said, "but don't ever try to repeat that deed."

Soon thereafter, the cap of the poor fisherman was full of money. Even the sailors of the Spanish galleons, who had seen his heroism, gave their coins.

Rufino was carried to his hut. Although seriously ill for some time, his strong constitution prevailed. He bought new fishing nets and a good boat. But he never returned to fight the monsters of the deep. From that time on, his long serrated dagger surrounded by shark teeth hung in his dining room.

Roberto Cofresi: The Pirate (1824)

The schooner *Ana,* tacking east and north-northeast, went around Boriquen's point and faced the angry waves of the Atlantic just beyond the quiet waters of Aguadilla.

"Tighten the foresail and let go the standing jib and the main," shouted Cofresí to his second mate. "Let's head for the high seas and see if we can find good fortune windward!"

The orders of the pirate were followed strictly. The light skiff, under full sail, traveled with increasing speed.

Waves broke with force against the bow, covering the deck with foam. Now and then the timbers creaked as the schooner surged forward, leaving behind a trail of greenish whitecaps and the fading silhouette of the island. The cool breeze from the northeast was steady. From time to time gulls dropped like handkerchiefs from the sky and flew over the boat crying.

"Pilichi, fetch me the spyglass," commanded Cofresí to the cabin boy. "I think I see something on the horizon."

Meanwhile, he put his hands over his eyebrows like a visor and with eagle-eyes searched the line where the sea met the sky.

When the telescope arrived, the pirate stretched it expertly. Then, sure of what he saw, with eyes flashing, he swung towards the bridge and shouted, "Mind the rudder, Galache, there is an enemy in sight."

A Danish brig was carrying merchandise from New York to St. Thomas. Even in those days that island, with its free port, was a great distribution center for European and North American cloth, hardware, and luxuries. The trusting merchant ship drew closer all the time.

Cofresí went to the bridge and ordered a bronze cannon loaded with powder and gunshot. He inspected it to be sure that both the gun-carriage and side-supports were standing strong and firm. Then he returned to the poop deck where the crew was gathering, and instructed each one of them personally. Machetes and knives were reviewed carefully, and more weapons were brought to the deck. All extra weapons were placed in a special area near the foremast. After these arrangements were finished, Cofresí calmly turned to sharpening his boarding axe with great care.

II

When the brig saw the schooner, it raised the Danish flag as a salute. The approaching pirate ship raised the skull and crossbones.

From the side of the brig ten riflemen lined up and fired. Their aim was poor and some bullets hit the sails of the *Ana,* while others hit the hull above the waterline.

While the musketry was reloaded, the pirate schooner came within seventy yards of the merchant ship and fired its cannon, startling the sailors of the brig. Before they could fire another shot, the *Ana* broached from the starboard, securing the brig with grappling hooks.

Cofresí, axe in hand, agile and swift, led the assault on the captive ship. The surprised defenders of the merchant ship were totally unprepared for hand-to-hand combat. After firing a few shots, most of the brig's sailors sought refuge below the deck.

Cofresí took charge of the ship quickly and killed the helmsman and the few merchant sailors remaining on deck. The hatches were closed, trapping the rest of the crew below. The Danish captain was found near the mainmast in a pool of blood, his head split by the blow of an axe.

After the corpses were thrown into the sea, and the decks cleared, the ship was plundered. A careful search was made below decks, and the trapped crew was tied up as each man emerged.

Before nightfall, the brig was scuttled. The pirate ship loosened its hold and idled by while the brig sank. Then it turned leeward toward the island and maneuvered around the point of San Francisco until reaching its hiding place in Cabo Rojo.

III

The merchants of St. Thomas were terrified at the plunderings of Cofresí. Finally, the United States Government took a hand in the affair and ordered the Navy to punish the Puerto Rican pirate.

But when Cofresí learned that an American man-of-war had been sent to help the insular authorities destroy him, he stopped his forays in the Atlantic and turned his attention to the Caribbean.

IV

While the *Ana* was at anchor at the point of Bocas del Infierno, a sail appeared on the horizon. Cofresí lifted anchor and promptly sailed to capture it. This time he got more than he had bargained for. As soon as he was within cannon reach, he was hit in the bow-sprit. Although he realized he was dealing with a warship, he went forward firing musketry and cannon, but his shots were promptly answered.

Recognizing the superiority of the warship, the schooner turned completely around and fled under full sail. Badly damaged, it raised a gaff-sail to make better use of the wind. Cofresí grabbed the tiller and by leading the schooner through shallows paralleling the coast, he was able to slip away from his pursuers. Once out of sight, he ran his ship aground on a sandbar. After loading the rowboats with as much booty as they would hold, the pirates rowed ashore.

V

Cofresí divided his men into two groups with plans to meet at the Cabo Rojo beach. Before separating, they buried the treasure brought ashore from the *Ana*. But a military patrol was searching the coast, and although each group divided and subdivided, they were trapped by the cavalry and had to surrender.

The pirate chief, seriously wounded, was captured only after a long, hard fight. To satisfy public demand, he was executed on March 29, 1825.

CARABALI:
THE REBELLIOUS SLAVE
(1830)

In the hills between Arecibo and Utuado, the traveler will find a grotesque cave. The base of the craggy mountain that contains this hole is reached through the picturesque plain where the Río Grande of Arecibo flows. On the flat, fertile farmland the sugar cane grows in tight bunches, while in the surrounding highlands, vegetation is scarce, and the scene dominated by royal palms, fruit trees, brambles, vines and ferns. On climbing a very narrow foot-path away from the main road one will see in the distance an immense rock with a somber spot — the entrance of "La Cueva de los Muertos" (The Cave of the Dead).

To enter this grotto, one has to crawl. Inside, the atmosphere is humid. It is difficult to see at first, but as the eyes adjust to the varied degrees of darkness, trails become apparent. Bats hover near the ceiling, and if a match is lit, the stalactites and stalagmites acquire a frightening, creature-like appearance. Opposite the entrance there is a wide fault which gives birth to a dark and bottomless chasm. A daring visitor looking over the rusty edge of the abyss will see nothing. He may become lightheaded from the humid breath exuding from the fissure. Everywhere the cavern has cracks caused by the subtle dripping of water on sandstone. The air is heavy-laden with dampness; the walls are covered with green minerals. The traveler is glad to leave this depressing ground littered with bones of animals and droppings of birds.

Years ago, one could see human skulls mixed with the animal bones, and for this reason the natives call the grotto "The Cave of the Dead." In early colonial days, the cave served as a refuge for slaves who escaped from the sugar mills. Because they had died in mortal sin, their souls were condemned to roam. Even today, they are said to meet in conclave on the night of San Blás to curse the owners of the sugar mill that carries this name. Today nothing is left of the sugar mill of San Blás except a pile of blackened chimney stones, and the memory of Carabalí, the Black deserter.

II

For the third time, Carabalí had escaped from the stocks in the jail of the sugar mill of San Blás. With the aid of darkness he had reached the highlands. The next morning, the guard reported the flight of the rebellious slave. The administrator let out a loud curse and immediately asked for the head foreman.

"Listen, Samuel," he said, "get the pack of hounds and gather whatever help you need to go after this accursed African who discredits us in front of the master. We have to set an example for all this trash. Bring him back dead or alive!"

III

The flight of the Black man was aided by the fog. The preceding day the fog lay only in the bay of the mill, but now it engulfed the factory's dormitories and houses. An old, lame Black woman out of work and disabled had helped the chronic deserter in his preparations. Now she lolled about the dining room while the stewards, seconds, and foremen sat around warming themselves with gin. The fog, at first light yellow like papaya, had slowly turned gray. The persistent drizzle soaked everything and changed the muddy ground of the square into a marsh. Sunset came very quickly, without the customary tropical preludes.

Carabalí crawled toward the edge of the woods and, once in the thicket, stood and took a deep breath. He could still see the torch near the mill through the dense fog, and angrily shook his fist at it. Eager to reach the protection of the dark cave he knew so well, he began to walk surefootedly towards the top of the mountain. The darkness, at first useful, now became a handicap. But his will to live stirred him onward. He knew that in the morning the foreman and dogs would be after him.

Carabalí entered the familiar cave like a snake. During his two previous escapes he had hidden there; he had

been captured only when, imprudently, he descended to
the plain. By feel, he searched on the ground near the
entrance. He rejoiced when he found some dry kindling
wood, and then proceeded to start a fire by rubbing one
piece against another. The light from the fire filled the
cave and disturbed some bats nearby, but the fugitive
felt at home. He was exhausted. He had climbed more
than a mile in order to reach the top. He took a piece of
tobacco from his pocket and after taking a bite he carefully put the rest away. As the fire grew dimmer, he
went to sleep.

V

It was a splendid morning. At the mill, everyone was
ready for the hunt. Samuel, the foreman, mounted his
horse and led the group, waving his cat-o'-nine tails. The
banana groves surrounding the buildings were searched
first, because in the past runaway slaves had hidden
there. But no trace was found.

"Let's divide into four groups," said Samuel, "we
must cover every inch of ground. Let the dogs go one
by one and guide them in the direction of the highlands.
We will all meet there and together comb the sugar cane
fields on our way back."

The hunt began. Like an avalanche the men and beasts
entered the thicket and swarmed through the shrubbery.
Only the lame Black woman remained in the otherwise
deserted square of the village. She looked at the hordes
of monsters with yellow bloodshot eyes and sardonic
smiles. She looked at these degenerates — more perverse

than the dogs — as they began the merciless pursuit of their unfortunate countryman.

VI

Carabalí opened his eyes as soon as the first light of dawn broke within the cave. He unfolded his stiff limbs and stretched himself out. He had slept all night crouched on a small pile of hay.

"Today for sure they will be after me," he muttered to himself. After thinking a while, he added, "So be it, my life will cost them dearly."

The lame Black woman had stolen a machete for him from a nearby storehouse. He sharpened it on a piece of sandstone. Then he scooped out a tropical gourd to use as a water cup, and breakfasted on some wild fruit.

"I will give them the trouble they are looking for," he muttered defiantly.

To test the sharpness of his blade, he neatly cut a bunch of vines hanging from the trunk of a tall ceiba.[1]

Then he began to chop down shrubs and branches to form a barricade at the mouth of the cave. Later he sat on a big stone nibbling on wild fruit, listening attentively for all sounds coming from the outside.

Suddenly, he heard barking dogs in the distance. He knelt for an instant with his ear to the ground, and then quickly stood up. The enemy was approaching: the barking of the dogs was getting louder and louder. He entered the cave and covered the entrance completely, leaving only a slight opening, the size of his hand, close to the ground. As the barking dogs drew nearer, he

1. A tropical tree

began to watch the entrance more carefully, chewing nervously on a bit of tobacco. Finally, the pack of hounds reached the mouth of the cave. The dog who arrived first stuck his head in the hole. As soon as he smelled the African, he began to force his entry. When one foot and all of his head had come through the hole, Carabalí chopped his head off. Then he replaced the branches the dog had pushed aside. In this way, he killed three of the ferocious animals, but the fourth he missed and merely cut the dog's mouth and an ear. The animal, howling violently, retreated to where the hunting party was. They saw the wounded dog and realized they had found their prize.

Before beginning the steep climb, the hunters fired their guns to frighten the fugitive. When they reached the cave, they fired their guns once more. Carabalí understood immediately that all was lost. The cave had only one entrance, and it would be impossible for him to fight against their firearms. Nevertheless, he swore not to surrender alive. He would skin alive whoever got in front of his machete.

The hounds barked furiously. The hole was enlarged. Two large dogs came through and rushed him. The fugitive kept them at bay with his machete. He cut the foot of one dog and wounded the flank of another. But the dogs began to surround him. A cunning bitch grabbed him by the calf. He let out a cry, and turning on his heels, he cut the bitch in two pieces with one blow. The anguished cry of the rebel was heard by his pursuers.

"Well, the bitch has caught her prey," said Samuel as

The hole was enlarged and two large dogs came through and rushed at him.

he lit a cigarette. Then, turning and grinning to his aides, he told them, "Go in quickly so that the dogs don't maim him or rip him into pieces."

Carabalí, anguished, tired, and wounded, stepped backwards towards the bottom of the cave. Suddenly, he fell into the chasm. The hounds stopped at the edge of the fault and began to bark continuously. When the foremen entered the cave, they approached the edge of the precipice in horror.

"Five hundred dollars lost," complained Samuel, furiously biting his tobacco. "I feel sorry for my dogs," said another foreman, "there was no one better to smell the mob and to grab them by their calves."

"There is a good side to everything," said another one of the pursuers. "Let's be glad we are rid of that agitator. He had all the slaves in the mill up in arms. Let him go to the devil."

"This breed of reddish Blacks is too proud," said Samuel. "They are no good for working in the fields. I have always told the master to buy Blacks from the Congo. They are humble, and very tolerant. Now let's return. The expedition has failed this time. Let's see how the supervisor will receive us. If the master gets angry, we may have to pay for the slave; maybe we will lose our jobs or receive a poor recommendation."

VII

Carabalí had fallen into a marsh from a height of 100 feet, and entered the mud like a gun into a holster — feet first and up to his waist. He was not injured. After recovering from the fall, he noticed that water oozed out of the cave through an opening, which allowed in a few rays of light. Carabalí reached the opening with great difficulty. Through it he saw the chimney of another mill — the San Antonio Mill. The mountain was the dividing line between the northern and southern haciendas. Carabalí recovered his machete and, straining his muscles, finally managed to climb out of the marsh.

A few days later, he descended into the valley and gathered many of the deserters of that area. They were all poor Africans who had been mistreated by their masters. The group worked together to carve a well-camouflaged staircase into the stone cliff within the cave. By this route they returned to rob the countryside near the San Blás sugar mill, while they lived unmolested in the lands of the other hacienda.

Carabalí and his gang terrified the foremen and supervisors of the San Blás hacienda. Many of their best workers were found murdered in the ravines. Government soldiers searched the countryside for the slaves, but when they entered the cave, they found nothing but bones of animals and human skeletons. After seeing this grim picture, they cautiously approached the mossy edge of the precipice. It seemed dark and impenetrable. In the San Blás sugar mill they came to think that the criminals did not really exist.

Encouraged by the shrewd, lame Black woman, the superstition arose that the hapless Carabalí came at night surrounded by other malignant spirits to kill the foremen and to steal the cattle and the fowl of the hacienda as offerings to Satan. During some clear nights, you could see thick smoke coming from the peak of the mountain. The guards interpreted this as signs of witchcraft and affirmed that Carabalí and his group were making sacrifices to the devil. The foremen, upon seeing the smoke, would make the sign of the cross and would ask everyone to keep away sorcery by praying a rosary.

Many years have gone by since these events took place, but this place is still called "The Cave of the Dead."

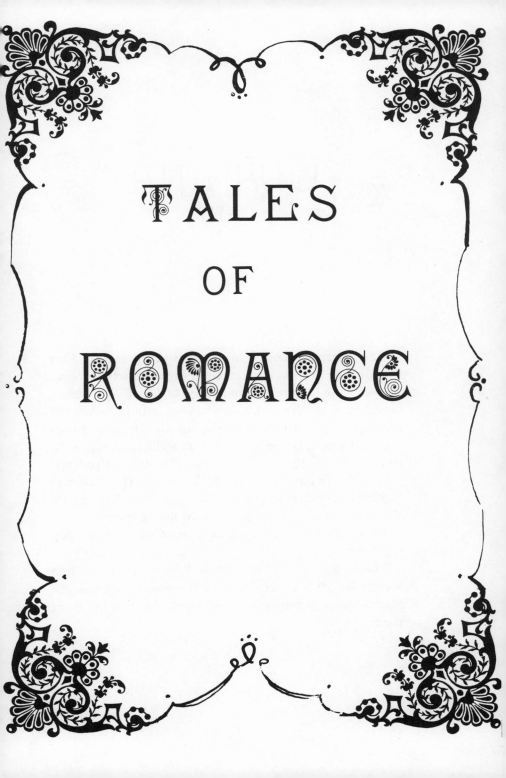

TALES

OF

ROMANCE

 GUANINA

(1511)

The afternoon ended in a sea of crimson, and Don Cristóbal de Sotomayor, seated in the comfortable room he had built in the Indian village of Chief Agüeybana, breathed with abandon the sensuous aroma which the breeze brought from the nearby woods. The young man was half-yearning for the court at Valladolid where he had left his mother, the countess of Camiña. Suddenly, a graceful Indian girl entered the room. Her hair was gathered in tresses in the old Castilian style. Her expressive eyes, filled with tears, betrayed her agitation.

"What has happened, my dear Guanina? Why are you frightened?"

"Flee, my lord! Flee, my dear love! Your death is sought by all the chieftains of Borinquen. I know the hidden caves in our island, and I will hide you in one of them."

"Are you delirious, Guanina? Your people are already conquered," answered Don Cristóbal. He drew the attractive Indian girl toward him and kissed her on the forehead.

"Do not believe, my lord, that my people are vanquished because my Uncle Agüeybana encouraged the natives of Borinquen to receive you with peace and with hospitality. The Indians believed then that you Spaniards were our brothers, but facts have shown differently. You are neither brothers nor friends; you seek to be our masters. Your people abuse our gentleness. The heavy work in the gold fields has made my people desperate. Some prefer to die by their own hand rather than to wash those accursed sands."

"I see, Guanina, that you also are rebellious," said Don Cristóbal, while seating her by his side and kissing her.

"I must tell you what I feel. I want to save you. I don't want you to die." Her eyes again filled with tears as she embraced the young nobleman who tried to comfort her.

II

It was then that Juan González, the interpreter, rushed into the room, cutting short the dialogue of the lovers.

"My lord, Don Cristóbal, there is no time to waste! A rebellion is at hand. It is overwhelming. I've just witnessed a war dance where your own subjects swore to kill you and to kill us all."

"You too have been frightened, my good Juan. Dismiss it. These are nothing more than emotional outbursts of slaves."

"For many nights," added the clever González, "I have seen light signals. I have heard the sound of alarm blown with seashells, echoing from mountain to mountain. I tell you the island is about to be consumed in a terrible race struggle. We must flee, my lord! We must flee! I know the shortcuts which lead to the city of Caparra. There is still time, my lord Don Cristóbal."

Loosening himself from the arms of Guanina, whose head was still gently reclining on his shoulder, the young man arose from the stool and shouted angrily, "Do you want to run away, Juan González? Don't you know my name is Sotomayor? When have you ever heard that a Sotomayor ran away from the enemy?"

"Tomorrow morning I will leave when the sun is high, with my visor up, my colors flying, with my friends and my retinue. My belongings will be on the backs of this mob that now fill the yard with their strident cries — this mob which soon will have to be punished. That is all, Juan, you may leave."

While the two Christians talked, Guanina walked to the window and looked with the piercing look of a savage creature into the darkening forest as if trying to discover its secrets. She finished braiding her handsome hair, mechanically, in the style she had learned from the young Spanish nobleman during their most intimate hours.

"Come, Guanina, sit by my side. I am angry with your people, but I am not angry with you. Your love fills my soul. Kiss me, Guanina, help me forget the anxieties that grieve me."

The Indian girl put her arms around the neck of the handsome youth and kissed him warmly.

III

The morning was brilliant. At sunrise, González, the interpreter, rapped quietly at the door of Don Cristóbal.

"My lord, my lord, it is I, Juan González."

"Come in. Good morning."

"We have kept watch all night while you slept. Let us leave, Don Cristóbal! Let us leave!"

"Call Guaybana, my chieftain-in-charge."

"I have already called him, my lord. He is at the front door waiting for your orders."

"Have him come in."

Juan González did as he was told, and Guaybana, the most important chieftain of the island of Borinquen, entered the room. The proud Guaybana greeted Don Cristóbal coldly, raising his right hand to a forehead which did not cease to frown. Guaybana had inherited the chieftainship from his Uncle Agüeybana; he hated the invaders with all his heart.

"Guaybana," commanded Don Cristóbal, "fetch me a group of your servants to take my belongings to the city of Caparra. I am ready and want to leave at once."

Juan González translated for his Captain.

"It will be done," answered the chieftain dryly, leaving the room abruptly.

"My lord, Don Cristóbal, what have you done?" asked

"It will be done," answered the chieftain dryly, leaving the
room abruptly.

the interpreter in anguish. "Why have you told Guaybana the route that we are to follow?"

"Juan, my good Juan, these idiots must know that we
are not frightened by them. Don't be afraid. The God of
Victories is with us. No one can insult the Castilian
standard. Go now, let's prepare for the trip."

The arrogant youth removed his Toledan sword, his
helmet and shield from the wall. Guanina approached
him and whispered softly: "Take me with you, my lord.
I do not want to remain without you. Take me with you!"

"Impossible, Guanina. As soon as we leave the village
there will be a battle. I don't want an arrow to hurt you.
A scratch on your skin would hurt me deeply. I will return for you soon, very soon. I promise you!"

Clasping her in his arms, he kissed her passionately.
Guanina cried quietly, but her muted sobs did not
change the plans of the reckless youth.

The Indian serfs poured into the room and distributed
the loads among themselves. They glanced at the crying
Indian girl with ill-disguised anger.

Don Cristóbal, wearing his helmet of burnished steel,
and with sword and shield in hand, kissed Guanina for
the last time. As he went out, he wiped with the small
finger of his left hand the trace of two tears which had
escaped from his loving eyes. This sign of weakness he
did not want his companions-at-arms to observe. The
tears were a just tribute of a proud Spanish champion to
the love of an Indian girl who, for his love, had sacrificed
the feelings that she had for her race.

The retinue waited on the square for last-minute

instructions. Juan González was ordered to the rear guard with the loaders while Don Cristóbal and his five friends guarded the front of the line against an ambush. The column was led by a good guide who frequently wandered ahead without protection. Since they went on foot they could not go fully armored. They wore only breastplates as protection from arrows.

IV

Soon after the retinue began its way through the freshness of the tropical morning toward Caparra, Guaybana gathered around him 300 of his best warriors and said to them:

"My friends, the hour of revenge has arrived. For many moons I have cried out about our misfortune. We must destroy all the invaders now, or die in the attempt. Our brothers from all regions of the island are already prepared for battle. The sun that shines today shines for us. The Great Spirit commands us to die killing. Do not be less courageous than the brave warriors headed by Guarionex and Mabo Damaca.[1] Aim your arrows and tie the straps of your clubs to your wrists. Now, press on, men — press on!"

Guaybana was wearing a multicolored feathered headgear; from his neck hung the guanín,[2] symbol of his authority. In his right hand he carried a heavy hatchet made of quartz with which he had leveled woods of cedar trees. The Indians were well armed, their quivers full of arrows; in the left hand they carried a bow, and in the right, a club. They wore their hair tied over the

1. Other Indian chieftains in the same struggle
2. A small sheet of gold worn by Puerto Rican chieftains

crown with a string of hemp. Their bodies were colored
with stripes made with a paste of yellow paprika and the
black juice of the jagua.[3] The Indians walked in disorder
down the same road which Don Cristóbal had taken
shortly before them. They talked and shouted, producing
an infernal babble; they had lost all fear of the foreigners.

V

The first one to sense the approach of the Borinquen-
ses on the warpath was Juan González. He ordered the
carriers to halt and search for the cause of the noise. But
just as he became sure of his premonitions, the Indians
jumped him. Two blows from the clubs cracked his skull
and covered him with blood. Fortunately, he did not
faint. He rushed to kneel in front of the proud chieftain
Guaybana, who had just arrived, and begged for his life,
offering to serve him forever.

"Leave the coward alone! Don't kill him!" said Guaybana. And turning arrogantly towards his warriors he
exclaimed: "Let us proceed towards Don Cristóbal and
his men!"

The Indian horde obeyed and trotted through a short
cut, shouting their war cries, while the bearers ran in
different directions after pilfering the cargo packs that
they had been carrying.

Once alone, Juan González gave thanks to God for
saving his life. He bandaged his head wounds the best he
could, and climbing a large and leafy tree, he waited
until nightfall to flee to Caparra. The interpreter pre-
ferred to play the role of Sancho Panza to that of Don

3. A tropical fruit

Quixote. He sacrificed his honor in order to save his skin. Despite his shame, the interpreter was deeply sorry he was unable to warn his master of the approaching avalanche.

VI

Don Cristóbal and his five friends walked cautiously. From time to time they heard strange and discordant noises coming from the woods. They moved through the trails, constantly on the lookout. Soon they realized that the Indians were coming towards them. The lookout at the head of the column stopped and gave the alarm. Don Cristóbal ordered his men to halt. With shields held tight and swords unsheathed, they turned in the direction from which the unintelligible voices were coming. From the streams of arrows they knew there were many enemies, and that the fight would be long and bloody.

"My friends," said the noble Don Cristóbal, "be ready to make your blows good. Although we are few, we are here to win. We must not drift apart, even for an instant. Be constantly alert, keep your feet on the ground and your shield ready for defense. Make each thrust straight and deadly. Keep your dagger in your left hand, and place your trust in God."

"Santiago and Sotomayor!" the Spanish soldiers shouted. "Santiago and Sotomayor!"

The Indian horde fell upon the small Castilian group like a river pouring over its banks at flood stage. The first Indians to arrive were killed at once; they had come upon the Christians so hurriedly that they could not use their bows and arrows. Soon, human blood covered the ground with a red hue; the air was filled with strident, angry shouts. The war cries of Don Cristóbal and his friends matched the screams of their adversaries. Brutally wielded Indian clubs were split in two by sharp Castilian swords.

The small Spanish group fought furiously, but harassment came from all sides. And while the Indians could be replaced, the Spanish could not.

Slowly the thunderous noise abated; breathing became labored. Everywhere, the ground was littered with bodies. The last one to fall was Don Cristóbal. He tried in vain to reach the proud Guaybana. But when he ran towards him, his sword was deflected by a woody vine. The first blow of Guaybana broke his sword, the next blow destroyed his life.

Guaybana and his warriors took shelter on a nearby hill to rest from the weariness of battle, to bury their dead, and to plan their campaign against the Christians remaining on the island.

The first to speak was the proud chieftain of Guainía.[4] "The Great Spirit is with us," he said. "My proud friend Don Cristóbal was courageous. He did not yield an inch. If we were cannibals, we would drink his blood to acquire his great courage. He must receive the honor due great warriors and be buried with ceremony suitable for a Spanish chief."

"Naiboa," he said to one of his men, "go to the head witch-doctor, Guacarí, and see that my orders are carried out."

When the adjutant Naiboa and twenty Indians went to retrieve the body of the unfortunate son of the Countess of Camiña, they found Guanina washing his face. In an insane delirium, she was trying to bring him

4. Village of chief Agüeybana, near the present town of Guaynilla

to life with her ardent kisses. The Indian delegation returned to Guaybana with the unhappy news that his sister would not allow them to touch the body of Don Cristóbal.

"So be it, Naiboa. The Great Guiding Spirit must have ordered it so," said Guaybana. "We will respect the anguish of Guanina, my friends. Tomorrow she will be sacrificed over the tomb of her lover, so that she may accompany him in the other life."

Sadly, he added: "Guacarí, you will carry out this cruel rite."

The witch doctor went with his helpers in search of the unhappy girl and the body of the Christian soldier, but when they arrived at the battlefield they found Guanina dead, her head resting on the bloody chest of the Spanish nobleman.

The bodies of Don Cristóbal and Guanina were buried at the foot of a large ceiba tree, and over this humble tomb, red poppies and white lilies grew -- nature's offering at the altar of love.

At sunset, when the purple light of the sun reddens the western slopes, the giant ceiba seems to be bathed in blood and its shadow shades a great expanse of land. The farmers nearby believe they can hear sweet songs of love in the gentle rustling of the leaves.

Since tradition has taught them that the courageous Don Cristóbal de Sotomayor and the lovely Indian Guanina were buried there, they believe that these young lovers return to view the evening stars and embrace in the moonlight.

THE DIAMOND RING
(1590)

"I am coming, my dear Mónica, to listen to you sing and play the guitar for a while."

"And what do you want to hear, Juanillo?"

"Why, the triumphal entrance of Don Gonzalo de Córdova into Naples. Also your imitation of the clarinets and trombones."

"Oh, you always ask for the same thing," she moaned.

"That is just the beginning; afterwards we can sing a bit."

"God forbid. You may be a good artillery man, but you sing terribly."

"But Mónica," pleaded the young man, "your divine voice enraptures me like the incense of the cathedral, and the strumming of your guitar saturates my soul. You can strike a martial air like the clash of two swords, or play a delicate piece as if you played to the Virgin."

"Flatterer, stop those falsehoods!"

"No! I swear it by the Virgen del Pilar of Zaragoza. I also want to tell you that last night I dreamt that I had given you a beautiful diamond wedding ring. And that after our marriage, we opened a stall to sell rum and orchata[1] in the marketplace."

"May heaven hear you, Juanillo! But, weren't you telling me a few nights ago that you were going to reenlist; aren't you the best artillery man in El Morro?"

"And I am, my love, but I'm tired of serving the King and living with the poor. And besides, I love you with all my heart."

II

Mónica was a marvel, always happy, full of life, and singing brisk and suggestive songs. She had a charming smile, and laughter like the jingling of silver bells.

Mónica loved Juanillo with childish coquetry. To check the enthusiasm of the military man, Aunt Brianda, who loved the girl as if she were her daughter, was always around. But all these jealous watchings were unnecessary because Juanillo had a noble heart.

Juan Alonzo Tejadillo (alias Juanillo) was a handsome Andalusian in his twenties and a charmer of females. In order to reach América, he had enlisted in Cádiz where he had mastered the ballistics of artillery.

III

A few months after the intimate dialogue we first related, the fleet of Sir Francis Drake appeared in front of San Juan with plans to seize the two million pesetas

1. An extract from a root used to make a refreshing beverage

in gold and silver that were aboard a flagship of the
Spanish colonial fleet then commanded by Sancho Pardo
y Osorio. Fortunately, five frigates of His Majesty's fleet
were also in the bay under the command of Tello de
Guzmán. All possible landing beaches were immediately
guarded, and the artillery was manned with anyone who
could shoot. The governor sent out warning messages to
Santo Domingo, Cartegena, and Santa María.

In those early days of 1590, San Juan was not a walled
city, and there was only one fort, Santa Catalina, later
to become the residence of the governor. El Morro was
not yet finished; it had a smaller stronghold next to it,
El Morrillo. In El Morro there were twenty-seven pieces
of artillery of the first order, among them a magnificent
high-caliber cannon given by Phillip II to this fort when
its construction was begun. The cannon had been captured by the brother of the King, Don Juan of Austria,
from the Turkish royal galley in the Battle of Lepanto
(1571). Juan Alonzo Tejadillo, the first artillery man of
El Morro, was in charge of the care and firing of this
special artillery piece.

Drake's fleet was formidable. He commanded twenty-
six ships, among them the *Defiance,* the *Judith,* the *Bon-
adventure,* the *Gardlant,* the *Hope,* the *Adventure,* and
the *Firefighter.* He dropped anchor at the entrance of
the bay, in front of the Island of Cabra.

After nightfall, he attacked the fort with twenty-five
well-armed landing craft. The attackers pressed forward
despite the artillery fire from El Morro and from other
batteries guarding the port. Primitive hand grenades and

incendiary bombs set afire the war frigates manned by
Tello de Guzmán while muskets and artillery peppered
the landing beaches. Bursts of fire from the burning
frigate *Magdalena* lit the bay. Aided by the light, the
cannoneers took better aim against the enemy landing
craft and forced them to retreat after a loss of ten boats
and more than four hundred men.

The first artillery man of El Morro saw the English
flagship near the entrance of the port and aimed his
Turkish cannon towards it. A light flickered with the
motion of the waves, through a window at the stern.
The gunner aimed directly at this light, made the sign of
the cross, and brought the linstock to the fuse. The
shell burst into the mess hall of the ship and killed John
Hawkins.

Drake loved Hawkins, his kinsman and master. Dis-
tressed by his death and the obstinate resistance of the
Spaniards, he lifted anchor the next day. People from
the towns of Arecibo and old San Germán sent the
cheerful news to the capital when they sighted the re-
treating British fleet.

The governor, Don Pedro Suárez, elated with the
enemy's defeat, gave the gunner, Juan Alonzo Tejadillo,
a diamond ring. The gift was given for "excellent service
to His Majesty and for having killed John Hawkins."

Juanillo gave the ring to his beloved Mónica. When
his enlistment period was over, he married her and
opened a stall to sell liquor and orchata in the Square of
the Verduras (today Baldorioty Square). Mónica, dizzy
with happiness, sold refreshments while proudly wearing
her diamond ring.

THE DAUGHTER
OF THE EXECUTIONER
(1765)

In the eighteenth century, *La Intendencia,* a beautiful building which lies facing the Plaza Baldorioty in San Juan, did not have the same artistic facade it has today. Its immense structure resembled the Bastille. *La Intendencia* was used as a prison; Plaza Baldorioty functioned as an open market.

The executioner was one of many persons living in this gloomy jail. He came to Puerto Rico with an appointment for life with his only living relative, a daughter ten years old. The child was raised by the wife of the warden who taught her and used her for the chores around the house.

María Dolores earned the good will of her protectress. She was as hard-working as she was humble and good.

María Dolores stood at the entrance of the prison with a pail of cool water

In the jail everyone loved her. Whenever the convicts returned from working in the fields María Dolores stood at the entrance of the prison with a pail of cool water to quench the intense thirst of the unfortunates.

In the early evening, the executioner was accustomed to accompany his daughter to say the rosary in the Church of Santo Tomás de Aquino (today the Church of San José). Afterwards he sat in the little square called Santo Domingo to enjoy the coolness of the night. The executioner spoke to no one. He lit his pipe and smoked while María Dolores walked around the square. After a while they returned to the prison by the way of Calle del Cristo.

As the years went by, María Dolores reached marrying age. She was appreciated by everyone for her Andalusian beauty and for her modesty. Although she wandered freely within the jail, no one uttered a coarse word in front of her. Her seriousness inspired respect. She continued to accompany her father to say the rosary with the Dominican friars, but now left the old executioner smoking in the small square while she took a long walk along the Street of San Sebastián. When she returned, she frequently had to wake her father, who dozed after his last smoke in the coolness of the late evening.

II

About this time a royal envoy, Don Alejandro O'Reilly, arrived at the capital to assess the conditions of this Spanish possession. One of his first official acts was to reorganize the National Guard and the Reserve. The city was greatly stirred by the increase in the enlistment notices.

Among those rejected for reenlistment was Betancourt, a handsome young man from the Canary Islands, a Private First Class who had demanded that he be made sergeant. When the captain of his company refused his unreasonable request, Betancourt came to complain to O'Reilly, but he behaved so rudely that the assistants of the royal envoy did not grant him an appointment. The arrogant young man then shouted:

"I was born to rule, not to be ruled . . . and rule I will!" And that very night he began to organize a gang of thieves which terrorized the city.

In those days the section of the Marina did not exist. This area later on was claimed from the sea and developed into a commercial section. At that time, there was only a narrow road that led to a tile factory, where the Arsenal is located today. The ships set anchor in front of the San Juan gate. The grocery and general stores were near the docks, in the open market now called the Plaza Baldorioty. The city was guarded by cavalry troops who made rounds through the streets to enforce a ten o'clock curfew. The streets were pitch black. Anyone that was found in the streets after ten was arrested, handcuffed, and taken to the House of Detention. (The system of having night watchmen came later.)

III

During one of her strolls in the Street of San Sebastián, María Dolores stopped to buy some caramels in a bakery called El Trueno ("The Thunder"), then located on the corner of San Justo Street. As she came out, a young man by the door exclaimed, "What a lovely figure. What beautiful eyes! You can't deny that you come from Cadiz,[1] because you stir up hearts wherever you go!"

María Dolores looked at the young man, smiled, and without losing her poise, she answered:

"Thank you, sir!"

She returned as usual to the square of Santo Domingo to accompany her father back to the prison.

The strolls continued and the encounters became more frequent under the calm and auspicious setting of the tropical nights. As fate would have it, the suitor of María Dolores was none other than the terrible bandit Betancourt, who had fallen madly in love with the attractive girl. After some months of courtship, he promised to ask for her hand in marriage, as soon as he finished his affairs in the capital. He then planned to move with her to one of the towns of the island and establish there a grocery store.

IV

The merchants complained repeatedly about the inadequacy of the protecting squads. Not a single night would go by without a store being robbed. O'Reilly took notice of this situation and advised the city government to double the watches and punish severely whoever was caught.

1. A part in southern Spain where people are known for their gaiety and expressiveness

One night, while one of the stores on the docks at the end of San Francisco Street was being sacked, a burglar was surprised and captured only minutes after killing two clerks. He was immediately taken to the hill of San Cristóbal, the hill where the fortified castle now stands, and after a summary trial, hanged. His corpse was left exposed to public scorn as an example for others. Since he was hanged at four in the morning, and was due to be brought down at the same hour the next day, there was ample opportunity for a huge populace to see the corpse of the bandit, and the city talked about nothing else all day long.

V

The tropical night was bright and without the slightest haze. María Dolores accompanied her father on his customary visit to the church and square. Once in the square she told her father:

"I would like to see the hanged man. It must be a horrifying sight!"

"What horrible taste, child!" said the executioner. "Think of something else. Take your usual stroll, and then let's go home."

"You are right, father."

And María Dolores, carrying around her waist her large multicolored kerchief, walked down the Street of San Sebastián. As usual, she bought some caramels at the baker's shop, but when she came out, she did not find Betancourt. Finding herself alone, she walked to the very end of the street. From there, she saw the gate of the city and felt again the desire to see the executed man.

"If Betancourt were here," she mused, "I would ask him to accompany me."

While she was thinking, the protection squad arrived, and the squad leader, who knew her, asked:

"What brings you here, María Dolores?"

"Sergeant, everybody has seen the hanged man. I have not, but my father does not wish to accompany me."

"Would you like someone in the guard to go with you?"

"No, it is still quite light out, I can even see the gallows from here. Let me just satisfy my curiosity and say an Our Father for the poor man. I'll be back in a moment."

María Dolores walked hurriedly. When she arrived at the gallows, she let out a horrified scream — a shaft of moonlight illuminated the face of none other than Betancourt! María Dolores quickly climbed the ladder used by her father to mount the gallows. When she touched him, the corpse was cold as ice, and she realized that he had been dead for a long time. In her distress, María Dolores lost hold of her senses. She took the shawl that was tied around her waist and tied it to the rope holding the bandit. Then, pushing the ladder aside, she hung by her neck while convulsively clasping the corpse of Betancourt.

VI

The old executioner awakened in the square of Santo

Domingo. He scrubbed his eyes and said:

"I have a feeling I have slept too long, but where's María Dolores?" As he walked and before he reached the baker's shop, he encountered the protection squad, who halted him.

"Who goes there?"

"The executioner."

"What are you doing out this late?"

"I am searching for my daughter."

"You cannot walk the street at this time of night without a special license. Do you have one?"

"No!"

"Then you are under arrest. Private Sánchez, handcuff the executioner and take him along."

As they approached the cathedral, the executioner felt that something had brushed against his face. He raised his eyes and saw a bat flying into the horizon. His eyes filled with tears. He was superstitious and interpreted this encounter as a sinister omen. When he was brought to the jail, the warden told him:

"It's three o'clock in the morning. Go ahead, bring down the man from the gallows at four and take him to the cemetery. We will discuss this other matter later."

Half an hour later the executioner was walking towards the hill of San Cristóbal. When he reached the site, he was terrified. With trembling hands he raced up the ladder only to find his daughter had been dead for some time. His body quaked as he descended. All at once the world around him began to spin, and he reeled like a drunkard and collapsed, dead from a sudden stroke.

VII

An immense crowd gathered around the scene of the tragic event. Even the governor and the bishop were present. No one could explain the mystery of the deaths of the executioner and his daughter, and some even believed that they had been killed in revenge by Betancourt's gang. After some time the owner of the bakery shop El Trueno let his customers know that the unfortunate María Dolores had been the girlfriend of the bandit Betancourt. Many skeptics, however, continue to believe that she and her father were the victims of revenge.

HISTORICAL TALES

A GOOD TOLEDAN SWORD[1]
(1625)

It was about the year 1625, and the truce between Spain and the Dutch Republic had expired. France, guided by Cardinal Richelieu, had joined with the Dutch against Spain. The Spanish king, Philip IV, was in the hands of his favorite minister, the Duke of Olivares, who, to flatter and control the monarch, offered him complete triumph over all his enemies. Although the Spaniards had recently won the battle of Fleurus, forcing the German Protestants to flee into Holland, more battles were raging in Flanders and in Germany.

At this time, the Dutch fleet chose to attack the Spanish possessions in América, looting the cities of San Salvador, Lima, and Callao. In those days, the city of Puerto Rico[2] was ignored by the crown. It had few troops, no walls, and none of the defenses which were built later, such as the heavily fortified castles of San Antonio, San Gerónimo and San Cristóbal.

1. Toledo is a town near Madrid famous for its excellent sword making
2. In those days, San Juan was called Puerto Rico

II

One morning in the month of September, the Dutch fleet appeared in front of the city with twenty-five boats. Taking advantage of the strength of the tradewinds, they crowded into the port at noon, their sails unfurled as if they were docking at their own shores in Holland. The artillery from El Morro fired haphazardly. Some artillery pieces at the castle were in such poor condition that with the first shot they fell from their gun carriages, while others had been loaded, but unused for years.

It was impossible to prevent the landing of such a formidable enemy. People who lived near the shore fled to the country. Even the military authorities took refuge in the fortress.

The enemy fleet was headed by General Boduino Enrico, an envoy from the Prince of Orange. He sent a page bearing a white flag to the governor, Don Juan de Haro to ask for the surrender of the fortress. The governor replied, "Had all the power of Holland landed, I should remain resolute. You shall never gain the keys of El Morro!"

Boduino Enrico ordered an immediate siege, and artillery pieces were placed in the plain that separated the castle from the city. The encirclement grew tighter every day, and finally the besieged were forced to make sudden sorties to cool the advances of the attackers. Despite this effort, the circle around the city became progressively smaller.

The Castilian chief rapidly advanced . . .

III

One morning, one of the detachments was so close to the boardwalks that one could distinguish the yellow feathers in the cap of the Dutch commander. The daring Dutchman was inspecting the moat and exploring the ravelins prior to storming the castle.

Suddenly, chains rattled, and the drawbridge dropped. A platoon of Castilians shot forth, headed by Don Juan de Amézquita, the Commander-in-Chief. The Castilian chief rapidly advanced on a brightly appointed spirited horse. One could hear the creaking of his spurless Cordovan boots, and the rippling of his chamois jacket. His Toledan sword, with a filigreed guard, caught the fierceness of the late afternoon sun. Its well-tempered steel blade bore the following motto: "Do not unsheath me without reason, or sheath me without honor." Seeing the advance of the Castilian chief, the Dutch captain surged forward. The troops from both sides fell back, leaving the opponents facing each other, waiting to see the fight of the two champions.

Physically, neither man had any advantage. It was apparent that both were well trained in weaponry. They did not cross their swords, but remained on guard with daggers at chest level. Their muscles were taut, ready to spring at any unprotected moment. A steady stream of heavy blows and surprising parries began. The silence of the onlookers was complete, and only the ring of clashing metal resounded. The Dutchman forced Amézquita to fall back and face the sun by astutely turning on his flank. Amézquita shrewdly yielded to the wishes of his contender: half closing his eyelids, he retreated and crouched. The Dutch captain, confident of the success of his maneuver to blind the Spaniard, lunged forward. Amézquita parried with the dagger, and guided his Toledan sword into the opponent's gullet.

The body of the champion of the House of Orange was carried in dismay back to the ship by his men. The Dutchmen put the city to the torch after looting the nearby houses. As they re-embarked, they were heavily bombarded by the stone catapults and wounded by the musketry. Before they left the port, they had lost some ships, and many men.

King Philip IV heard of the great bravery of the Puerto Rican captain, Don Juan de Amézquita y Quixano, and rewarded him with one thousand crowns, a promotion, and the governorship of Santiago de Cuba. But Don Juan resigned this post a few months later to return to his native land.

In the courtyard of El Morro, there is a monument that commemorates this event — the name of the heroic Puerto Rican does not appear.

The Eleven Thousand Virgins
(1797)

In 1797, after conquering Trinidad with a squadron of sixty ships, Abercromby, the British general, turned toward Puerto Rico and landed his well-trained troops on the beach of Cangrejos, near the capital.

The country was then ruled by General Don Ramón de Castro, who prepared the city for attack. The bridge of San Antonio was rendered impassable. Dinghies were gathered, pontoons were built, artillery pieces were placed in several small boats. A mounted patrol was enlisted to explore and defend the nearby countryside from the looting of the enemy. Women, children, and old people were evacuated from the city. Only the men who could carry arms remained.

The landing of the British troops could not be prevented. The British ships that laid anchor in the inlet of Cangrejos protected the landing at the beach of Torrecilla with heavy artillery fire.

Having established his command in the Bishop's residence, near the Church of San Mateo, Abercromby headed west. At the bridge of San Antonio, heavy artillery fire from a small fort nearby, and from the fort of San Gerónimo, stopped his advance. Trenches were dug in the Miramar section of the Condado and heavy artillery fire was equally exchanged. The British siege began on the 17th of April. By the 29th of April, the situation had not changed. The assailants and the besieged had fought to a standstill.

II

Trespalacios, Bishop of the diocese, sent ecclesiastical delegates everywhere in the garrison, even to the areas of maximum danger and, in addition, sent money for the defense of San Juan.

On the 30th of April the quartermaster of the city sought the Bishop. "Your Eminence," he said, "why don't we organize a public supplication?"

"An inspired thought!" said the Bishop. "We will make a mass petition to St. Catherine, the patroness of the fort built in this city, and we will petition St. Ursula and the Eleven Thousand Virgins, to whom I am very partial."

"And how will the procession be organized?"

"Why, the whole city will take part in it," answered the Bishop. "Whoever doesn't have a candle made of beeswax will carry one made of tallow, and the very poor can carry wooden torches. The hierarchy, myself, and the civil authorities will head the procession, which will leave the cathedral in the late evening and march through all the streets of the city. At dawn, we will return to the church for a pontifical mass with a full orchestra."

And so it began. The bells in all the churches were rung.

III

At nine o'clock in the evening, the English lookouts advised the headquarters of Abercromby that a great deal of commotion was noted in the city. The church bells were ringing, and the western part of the city was all illuminated.

"They must be receiving reinforcements from the countryside," said the British general. "Unfortunately, my frigates cannot get any closer because of the heavy artillery fire from the fort."

He then ordered that intense musketfire be directed to the trenches of the Condado, and against the small boats that defended the city with their artillery.

At midnight, the general was again notified that the number of lights in the city were growing and that now they were moving eastward.

Abercromby then gathered his chiefs of staff and told them: "We have been here for nearly a month and we control only what we obtained the first day. This fortress is well defended; dysentery is beginning to take its toll amongst our troops. Reinforcements from the countryside are arriving at the city, and it is plain we cannot prevent their entry. Undoubtedly they are preparing tonight for a great counterattack against our encampment. I believe, therefore, that we should return to our ships."

The staff concurred. The order to load the ships was given, and by dawn, the first of May, the siege was over.

IV

In the cathedral, the Te Deum was sung after the high mass, and later the Bishop preached. My great uncle, a lieutenant who had arrived with a company from Arecibo on the 22nd of April, talked about the great triumph of Santa Ursula and the Eleven Thousand Virgins. My grandmother, who died at the age of 97, heard the whole story from him. She heard that on that memorable night the enemy artillery fire had been intensified and that the bullets, halfway through their course, turned against the assailants. When the great procession entered the cathedral, the cannon fire suddenly ceased and the enemy disappeared.

I believed this story for a long time. But when I learned that St. Ursula and the Eleven Thousand Virgins were British, I began to think that if they had come at all to help, they would have rather helped their own.

Tales of
Religion
and
Superstition

The Miracle of Hormigueros (1640)

In the household of Gerardo González, everyone was in despair. María Monserrate, the golden dream of her father, the one who brought happiness to his home, had disappeared. "Monsita" was eight years old. She had clear eyes, the color of the heavens, and fair skin, a blend of roses and lilies. The whole neighborhood shared the grief of González. Friendly farm-hands and wealthy ranchers searched for her through the hills and the wilds of the nearby sierra.

Two weeks after her disappearance, they found her seated, whispering a tune inside a big hole at the base of a large ceiba tree.

II

Don Gerardo, both laughing and crying at the same time, asked her: "But my love, weren't you afraid of the darkness?"

"She was beautiful, and her skin was black, like coffee."

"No, Daddy. Here at night there is a gentle light which pours out of that cave."

"But, my sweet, weren't you hungry?"

"No, Daddy. From that same cave, a lady dressed in white came forth to give me delicious fruit and to caress my face with her perfumed hands."

"Did you see her face? Do you know her? Who does she look like?"

"She had bright, black, gentle eyes and she smiled at me. She was beautiful, and her skin was black, like coffee."

"She is my patroness!" exclaimed Don Gerardo, full of joy and faith. "Blessed be her name forever and ever . . . !"

III

Gerardo González founded the Chapel of Our Lady of the Monserrate among the rolling hills of Hormigueros in 1640. The Viceroy placed the Chapel and Monastery under his care.

The church of the Monserrate still stands, and the petitions in the Chapel are proof that our solid faith has not been completely lost. There is still devotion in our hearts to give honor to those thick walls and to bring flowers to the black Virgin who helped little María Monserrate.

The Church of Christ the Healer (1766)

In San Juan, where Tetuán Street joins the end of the street called Calle del Cristo, there remains an unused chapel supported by a Roman arch that obstructs the road. The weathering that comes with age gives this small church the appearance of a historical monument.

When the chapel was built in 1753, the Calle del Cristo was the race track of the period. The steep hill had no sidewalks or cobblestones. It was sandy in some places, muddy and full of holes in others. The riders gathered in front of the city wall, and two at a time, they would race toward the Dominican Convent. The finish line was the St. Thomas Aquinas Gate, today known as the San Jóse Gate. The riders would then trot back to the starting line, competing with each other in the rocky descent of the incline.

One afternoon, a group of youths returning to the starting line pressed their spirited horses into a rapid gallop. One of the horses, ridden by the daring youth, Baltazar Montañez, lost control and bolted over the wall into the chasm. The Secretary of State, General Don Tomas Mateo Prats, who watched the race from a balcony, cried out an anguished plea, "Save him, Christ the Healer! Save him!"

The horse was torn to bits among the rocks, but the youth escaped unharmed . . . .

And so it was that Señor Prats, being a devout man, built the Chapel on top of the wall and placed there an image of Christ the Healer. As time went on, this image was said to have miraculous powers, and for many years, great religious feasts were celebrated in honor of it.

Now, only the ruins remain . . . .[1]

1. Since this story was originally written the Church of Christ the Healer has been completely restored

The Bell
of the Sugar Mill
(1840)

At one time the ancient sugar cane Hacienda of Rancho Viejo had its powerful grinders turned by oxen. But in 1830 with the acquisition of a steam engine and more land, it became the important sugar mill of San Jorge. Don Jorge Smith developed the large hacienda in the Jamaican fashion, with quarters for many slaves. There was little left of the primitive buildings except the old mill and a circular tower of heavy masonry, which became the watchtower for the farm; there a large bell was hung to awaken the slaves at dawn.

When the bell was rung three times, the slaves left their locked and well-guarded quarters and headed for their jobs under the custody and supervision of a second foreman. A second tolling of the bell signaled the end of cultivation and a rest from heavy labor in the sugar mill and distillery. The same metallic ring called them back to work.

As the years went by, new bells replaced the old ones as they cracked. The shrill whistle of the steam engine finally superseded the outmoded instrument. Time was then regulated by Swiss watches which became plentiful and cheap; even the heavy clock of the sitting-room with its elaborate weights and balances gave way to a small eight-day clock.

Don Jorge, the founder of this Hacienda, had only one heir — his niece Doña Carlota. She immigrated from Jamaica and married Don Conrado, the first superintendent of the mill, one year after settling in Puerto Rico.

One hot summer night as Doña Carlota lay awake reading, she heard quite clearly the old bell of the mill gently tolling. First she thought it was only the wind, but as the low-pitched metallic sound distinctly recurred, she became positive that it was made by the cracked bell of the mill.

Doña Carlota told no one but her husband about this incredible occurrence, and even he never quite believed the story. But she vividly recalled it the next day when her uncle died suddenly of a stroke.

After Doña Carlota inherited the Hacienda, the doors of the old mill were sealed completely "so that no one could hide in the place."

II

Doña Carlota and Don Conrado had three sons and a daughter. For a long time they enjoyed the benefits of the productive sugar mill. But once again, on the eve of her twenty-fifth wedding anniversary she heard the sound of fate at her door. It was late in the evening as she prepared cream puffs and cakes for the next day while waiting for the return of her husband from town. Suddenly she heard the cracked bell of the mill. She hastened to her bedroom and gazed through the open window into the stillness of the cool night. She began to pray, but halfway through her prayers the rosary dropped from her hands as she heard again the soft metallic ring. Frightened, she slammed the window shut and lay in her bed without undressing. The arrival of morning brought no relief to her anguish — not until three o'clock was Don Conrado brought back to the mill on a stretcher. A rebellious slave, who had been cruelly punished by a foreman, had taken vengeance on the weak master. Behind the rosebushes of the garden, he had cut him to death.

III

Many years went by. The sugar mill of San Jorge was preparing for the wedding of Stephanie, the sixteen-year-old daughter of Doña Carlota. An elegant wedding was planned. Negro slaves were to be baptized by white people from high society. The mulatto woman who nursed Stephanie when her mother fell ill, and the old Negro man who took her to school as a child were to be freed. The celebrations were to last two days and two nights. On the morning of the third day the wedding would take place, and the newlyweds would take advantage of the coolness of the morning to make their way to the capital in time to board the intercolonial steamer

Doña Carlota gazed through the open window into the stillness of the cool night and began to pray.

heading for St. Thomas. From St. Thomas a transatlantic
ship would take them to St. Nazaire and the beginning
of a long European tour.

During the first day the festivities were very lively.
The baptisms were done in the morning; the afternoon
dance lasted until midnight. After the dance, Doña Carlota sat on a swing in her bedroom to watch the moon
rise over the sky of her open window. A cool wind was
blowing from the sugar cane fields, and her mind was
filled with happy recollections of the past. It was one
o'clock. She rose swiftly to close the door of her
room before retiring, but froze in her steps: the vibra-
tions of the cracked bell had caught her ear. She dropped
to her knees, and heard again the dull ring of the cracked
bronze. Lifting her eyes to the sky, she wept and prayed:

"Oh my God, what misfortune is awaiting us now?
Let me be the victim this time!"

IV

The next day was radiant, not a single cloud in the
powdery blue sky. At breakfast the men made plans to
go hunting for ringdoves in the nearby palm forest.
When breakfast was finished, the young women played
the piano, the guitar, and the mandolin. They sang
guarachas[1] for a while, but finally became bored. They
missed the encouragement of the young men to sing and
dance. Stephanie, the bride, proposed a dip in the nearby river. There they could pass the time beneath the
bamboo trees or in the cooling waters.

The troop of lovely girls headed for the river accom-

---

1. A Caribbean dance still popular in Latin America

panied by trusted servants. The young girls ran down the banks of the river and spilled with abandon into the swift but quietly moving waters. The first one to lose her foothold screamed and pulled others towards her. Although the maids were excellent swimmers, four of the youths including beautiful Stephanie drowned. When the fatal news reached Doña Carlota, she fell to the ground as if struck by lightning. She recovered consciousness sobbing and screaming with anguish, cursing the old bell of the mill.

V

Years passed. One night near midnight Doña Carlota heard once again the somber metallic chiming. The following morning, having a foreboding of death, she gathered her sons and told them quietly her painful story. By the afternoon she was dead.

Was Doña Carlota having hallucinations? Were the deaths and the tolling of the bell merely happenstance? How many secrets we have yet to learn from nature.

HISTORICAL NOTES

HISTORICAL NOTES

On November 19, 1493, Columbus landed in Puerto Rico between the present towns of Aguada (watering place) and Aguadilla (little watering place). He found an island, approximately 100 miles long and 35 miles wide, of green and exuberant vegetation, rolling hills, and forests abounding in tropical fruits. He encountered small and peaceful native communities with a stable social and political structure, whose people lived by farming and fishing. Men and women generally wore no clothing. They were of medium height, a pale matte complexion, slanted eyes, and thick straight hair sometimes tied high on top of their heads.

The Taínos were a blend of North and South American Indians, the more primitive *Arawak* and the culturally more advanced *Igneri.* The original Indian settlers came from the Floridian coast before the Christian era. They mixed with migrants from the northern coast of South America around the tenth century A.D. These gentle people were in harmony with a generous and unexacting environment. Their natural enemies were the savage and cannibalistic Caribes who came from smaller neighboring islands to pillage and destroy the Taíno villages and steal their women.

Colonization was begun in 1508, two years before the first settlement on the North American continent at Jamestown, Virginia. Juan Ponce de León left the first settlement in the Western Hemisphere on the island of Hispaniola, landing in the beautiful and well-protected bay of Guánica, the same bay chosen by the American expeditionary force in 1898. Ponce de León met with Agüeybana, the most important chieftain of *Boriquén* (Puerto Rico) who granted the Spanish chief the title of guatío (blood brother) and offered him any area of his choosing as his dwelling place. Ponce de León founded Caparra on the Northern Coast near the present city of San Juan.

The harmonious relationship between the Spanish and the Taínos lasted less than a year. Land grants and groups of forty Indians (known as *encomiendas*) were divided among Ponce de León's high officers. The Indians were forced to work mines and pan rivers for gold for the benefit of the Spanish settlers. Spaniards were thought to be gods until 1511 when the old chieftain Urayouan from Añasco ordered Diego de Salcedo submerged in the river. The drowning of Salcedo demonstrated that the Spaniards were mortals and that a fight for survival had a chance of success. "The Gold Nugget" brings forth the adventuresome spirit and greed of the early Spanish settlers. The betrayal felt by the Indian and the nobility of the Taíno spirit is portrayed in the love story "Guanina."

Arrows and clubs used by the Taínos to fight the man-eating Caribes were no match for the firearms, swords, horses, and dogs which the Spanish possessed. In less than 5 years the Indians were reduced to slavery.

In 1519 the capital of the island was moved to its present site because of malaria and other pestilences found in the marshes. As gold became scarce, sugar-cane was introduced to the island and slaves from Africa were imported to take the place of the fast-disappearing Taínos. The first sugar mill was installed in San Germán in 1523. Sugar cane remained Puerto Rico's leading cash crop until nearly the present day. In "Carabalí" we perceive the Puerto Rican version of the infamy of slavery.

San Juan's dominant position as an outpost of the Spanish empire began in 1533 with the construction of La Fortaleza, the residence of Puerto Rican governors for the last four centuries. The impressive fortress of El Morro was functional enough by 1590 to ward off an invasion by Sir Francis Drake as described in "The Diamond Ring." Holland, recognized as an independent country since 1609, demonstrated its rising sea power by its forays in the new hemisphere; one of them is narrated in "The Good Toledan Sword." The final assault of the British occurred under General Abercromby in 1779, an event that led to the fanciful tale of "The Eleven Thousand Virgins."

San Juan grew to become one of the leading stepping stones between the Spanish-American empire in the Western Hemisphere and the Iberian Peninsula. Its sophisticated fortifications were considered second only to the ones in the seaport of Cartagena, Columbia. Since the Spanish crown refused to establish legal trading arrangements between Denmark, England, France and other unfriendly countries, miles of unprotected Puerto Rican beaches became an open market for smugglers and pirates. The easygoing fashion with which smuggling and piracy were contemplated at the time are only partially portrayed in the short legend "Cofresí: The Pirate."

In 1850 Puerto Rico had 500,000 people. There was a mixture of Spanish, Indian and African, but the French, English, Dutch, Italian, and Corsican stock were also represented. By 1897 the population had grown to 900,000. Luis Muñoz Rivera led the political forces that persuaded Spain to grant a measure of autonomy to the island from the Spanish crown, an event that lost its practical significance with the American occupation on July 25, 1898. The years of American colonialism ended officially on July 25, 1952, when the Commonwealth of Puerto Rico was established under the leadership of Muñoz Marín, Muñoz Rivera's son.

The Commonwealth status gave Puerto Rico some of the attributes of a state.

Puerto Rico controls completely its schools, police, courts, public works and internal communications. It has a bicameral legisla-lature. It is represented in the United States House of Representatives by a Resident Commissioner elected by the people for a four-year term. This Commissioner votes in the House committees to which he belongs but has no vote on the floor of the House. Since we have no vote in the United States Congress, we are exempt from federal taxation. The Federal Government retains control of customs, interstate trade, the post office, the coast guard, the armed services, and the licensing of radio and TV stations. The Puerto Rican judicial system has access to the federal judicial system through the Court of Appeals of Boston.

In 1967 Puerto Ricans voted overwhelmingly in favor of maintaining a Commonwealth status, but now there is a growing interest in statehood. Some have serious concerns about losing their cultural identity if Puerto Rico becomes the fifty-first state, while others see the Commonwealth as a colonial vestige offering second-rate citizenship. Less than ten percent of eligible voters favor independence. Any change in political status must have the consent of the United States Congress and the Puerto Rican people.

IMPORTANT HISTORICAL EVENTS

1493   Columbus lands near the town of Aguadilla on November 19.

1508   Ponce de León becomes first governor of the island.
Cristóbal de Sotomayor founds the city of Sotomayor in Aguada.

1511   The Indians kill Cristóbal de Sotomayor. Ponce de León attacks the main Indian city of Guaynía near the present town of Guanica killing Guaybana and crushing the rebellion.

1809   The Supreme Council recognizes the American colonies as an integral part of Spain.

1868   A small group of rebels captures the western town of Lares and proclaims the Republic of Puerto Rico on September 23. The next day they attack the town of San Sebastian and they are dispersed, killed or imprisoned.

1873   Slavery is abolished.

1876   The Puerto Rican Ateneo is founded by Manuel Elsaburu initiating the cultural awareness still manifested today.

1895   The Cuban rebellion begins. Puerto Ricans in New York collaborate pushing forth for Puerto Rican independence.

1897   Spain concedes Puerto Rico a measure of autonomy.

1898   U.S. infantry unloads 633 men in Guantánamo on June 10 thereby initiating the Cuban invasion. Fifteen days later, July 25, U.S. troops enter Puerto Rico through Guánica.

The Treaty of Paris is signed on December 10. Spain agrees to surrender Puerto Rico and other islands under Spanish dominion in the West Indies, and the Island of Guam in the Marianas.

1900   The American Congress recognizes Puerto Rico as an unincorporated territory with its governor to be designated by the President on April 12. Only the President can override the governor's veto. The legislative branch composed of an executive committee of 11 members designated by the President and a chamber of delegates of 35 members elected by popular vote is authorized. The position of Resident Commissioner to represent Puerto Rico in the Congress of the United States with voice but no vote is also established.

1917   Puerto Ricans are granted American citizenship and required military service. The legislature is reorganized into a senate of 19 members and a house of representatives of 39, both elected by the people. A governor appointed by the President of the United States with the power of absolute veto is retained.

1935   President Roosevelt by executive order establishes on May 28 the Puerto Rican reconstruction administration which begins an ambitious program of public works, electrification and agricultural development.

1936   Senator Millard E. Tidings of Maryland initiates a congressional proposal to grant independence to Puerto Rico on April 23.

1940   The Popular Democratic Party founded by Luis Muñoz Marín gains control of the Senate by one vote.

1941   Rexford Guy Tugwell, ex-Subsecretary of Agriculture of the United States and Chancellor of the University of Puerto Rico, is named governor of Puerto Rico. This gives Puerto Rico an American governor well acquainted with its problems.

1944 The Senate of the United States approves unanimously a bill authorizing the Puerto Rican people to elect their own governor. The Popular Democratic Party initiates its policy of "Operation Bootstrap."

1946 President Harry S. Truman designates a native-born Puerto Rican, Jesús T. Piñeiro, as Governor of Puerto Rico.

1947 The United States Congress recognizes the right of the Puerto Rican people to elect their own governor.

1948 Luis Muñoz Marín is elected governor of Puerto Rico. Of 168 previous governors of the island, Munoz Marin is the second native-born Puerto Rican to hold this post.

1952 The commonwealth of Puerto Rico becomes officially established on July 25.

1955 The Institute of Puerto Rican Culture is created for the dissemination of our culture and traditions.

1956 The Casals' Festival initiates a renaissance of classical music and the arts in general.

1959 Luis A. Ferré, wealthy industrialist, establishes the first Museum of Fine Arts in Puerto Rico in Ponce, with his personal art collection.

1960 Following the trajectory initiated by Pablo Casals, the Conservatory of Music is established. Native talented musicians of modest means can now achieve artistic refinement.

1968 In a tight political race Luis A. Ferré becomes governor of Puerto Rico as leader of the pro-statehood party, the New Progressive Party. This is the first change in government in 28 years. It revitalizes the electoral process offering an alternative to the Commonwealth.

1972 The Popular Democratic Party returns to power. An attempt to broaden the powers of the Puerto Rican government while maintaining the structure of the Commonwealth fails.

1979 The Pan-American Games take place in San Juan. Athleticism flourishes. Plans are made to try and bring the world Olympics to Puerto Rico in 2004.

1981 Opening of the Center of the Performing Arts. Outstanding virtuosos and world-renown performers add San Juan to their itineraries.

1986 Juan Pablo II stages the first papal visit to the island. There is a resurgence of religious interest, particularly among young people.

1988 By establishing commercial agreements of mutual benefit with other countries of the Caribbean Region, Puerto Rico increases its role as a link between the United States and spanish-speaking nations.

1992 As part of the anniversary celebration of five centuries since the European discovery of the Americas, seventy sailing ships from nearly as many nations arrive in San Juan. The handsomely attired port, with its neighboring tree-lined walks and plazas, are an appropriate tropical setting for open-air festivities.

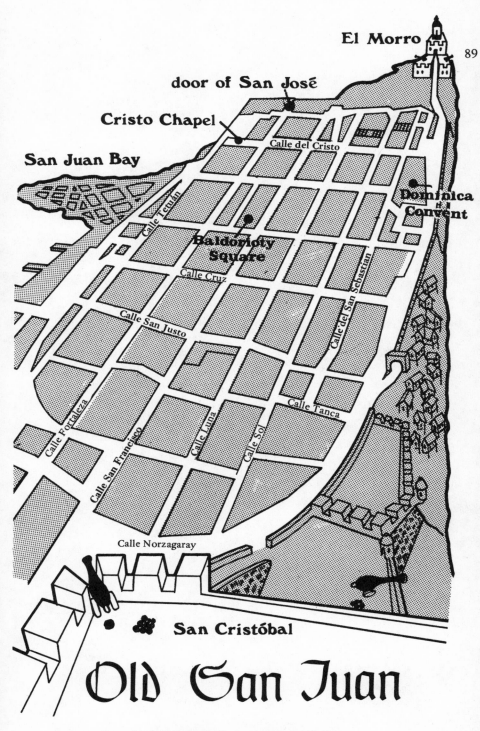

El Morro

door of San José

Cristo Chapel

Calle del Cristo

San Juan Bay

Dominica Convent

Calle Tetuan

Baldorioty Square

Calle Cruz

Calle del San Sebastian

Calle San Justo

Calle Tanca

Calle Fortaleza

Calle San Francisco

Calle Luna

Calle Sol

Calle Norzagaray

San Cristóbal

Old San Juan

Streets mentioned in the legends in bold type.

ABOUT THE AUTHOR

Cayetano Coll y Toste was born in Arecibo in 1850 and died in Madrid in 1930. After receiving his bachelor's degree from the Jesuit College in San Juan, he migrated to Barcelona, earning a doctorate degree in Medicine in 1874. While there he founded and directed *El Ramillete,* a literary weekly. His *magnum opus* was the *Historical Bulletin of Puerto Rico (Boletín Histórico de Puerto Rico),* a fourteen volume collection of notes dealing with pre-history, colonial history, public education, economics, political development and other aspects of Puerto Rican life. Just before the American occupation of Puerto Rico, in 1898, he was Secretary of Agriculture and Commerce and Secretary of the Treasury. During 1924-1925, he published three volumes of stories based on historical facts and folklore under the title *Puerto Rican Legends and Traditions (Leyendas y Tradiciones Puertorriqueñas).* Twelve of these stories are translated here.

To: Marina Muñoz
The most Important Little
person in My life.

8/ 94

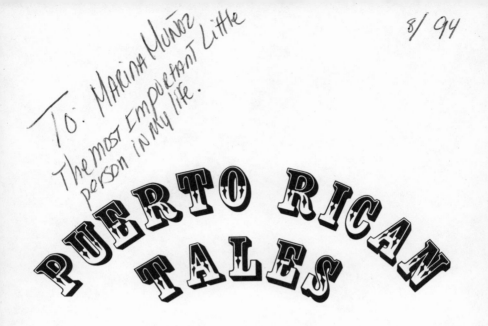

PUERTO RICAN
TALES

Love
Mom.

"The three volumes of stories based on historical facts and folklore, *Leyendas y Tradiciones Puertorriqueñas,* by Cayetano Coll y Toste (1850-1930), compose a literary classic. Now, for the first time, twelve of those stories have been brilliantly translated into English and published in a book."

—X.M.
NUESTRO
THE MAGAZINE FOR LATINOS

"This collection of legends translated in English will doubtlessly serve our compatriots (Puerto Ricans in the U.S.) as an effective means to delve into the same historical source offered to those of us who were raised in Puerto Rican classrooms, reading the original Spanish version of the stories of Coll y Toste . . . We congratulate wholeheartedly the author of these translations. All Puerto Ricans conscious of our cultural heritage rejoice unabashedly in his achievement."

Manuel Alvarez Nazario
Professor of Hispanic Studies
University of Puerto Rico

Borinquen point

Guajataca

Arecibo

Aguadilla

Aguada

Rincón

Utuado

COR

Mayagüez

Maricao

Sierra de Guilarte

Hormigueros

Basilica de Monserrate

Guainía

Ponce

Guánica

Parguera

Cabo Rojo

Caribbean Sea

Puerto